SALES SYSTEM MASTERY

CARL HENRY

ONE

Every Sale Has a Roadmap

Many years ago, when I was still in school, I found myself fascinated by the stories I heard about explorers and adventurers in history class. These were people who dreamed of far-off places and – without the benefit of engines, radar, or GPS devices – simply set off sailing until they either found a place they hadn't been before or disappeared into thin air. Even then, the idea that someone would load up a boat with things like water and salted meat and simply hope for the best seemed pretty incredible.

As interesting as it might have been, it was hard to believe anyone would risk their lives without even knowing where they were headed.

I still think about those stories from time to

time. This is partly because my work as a sales coach, trainer, and keynote presenter takes me across North America, and even overseas, on a regular basis. The pilots and drivers I meet are our modern-day captains, and I even have to strike out on my own through unmarked county roads in a rental car from time to time.

What reminds me of those intrepid explorers even more, though, is the way so many salespeople seem to work. I've met new and seasoned professionals in hundreds of industries. I've gotten to speak with them in offices, bullpens, and conference rooms every year for decades. What I've learned along the way is that the best are always following a systematic plan that leads them toward sales success. They don't leave things to chance.

The best salespeople know, as I do, that every sale has a roadmap. There is a beginning, middle, and an end. Going from start to finish can take a few minutes or several years, but there is almost always a process that has to be followed. If you ignore that reality, you set yourself up for a lot of stress and missing commission checks.

To put things another way, you aren't going to make very many sales by accident. Nor are you likely to "wing it" and earn a huge consistent income. If you want to guide customers from their first contact to the finished sale again and again, you should be following a proven sales system. In the coming pages I'm going to show you why you need one, how to choose one, and the best ways to make it work.

This short book is unlike any of the others I've written. Not only is the structure different than I'm used to, but the short chapters aren't designed to teach you a specific skill. Instead, it's set up to get you thinking about the importance of a sales system, show you why you need one, and help you to find a plan that will work for you.

Naturally, I'm hoping you'll settle on something like my *MODERN Sales System*, which is currently being used by many top producers in well-known companies around the world. However, the truth is I'd rather have you using *any* sales system than none at all. The stakes are just too high.

There was a time when it made sense for people to head off in new directions to parts unknown without being sure what they would run into. And, selling might have been new enough at one point for producers to feel like they could succeed by just making things up as they went along. However, both of those eras have passed. You can't walk into an airport and buy a ticket to "anywhere." You have to choose a destination. Likewise, we know enough about selling, and the buying process, to see that you should be guiding prospects through an orderly, step-by-step process.

The bad news is that learning a sales system takes a little bit of work and might force you to change your behavior or ignore your instincts. The good news is that as your new habits sink in, your life will get easier and you'll make more money than you ever have in the past.

If you're willing to work like a true sales professional – and be paid like one – let's get started. The first thing you need to know is just how important a sales system can be to your success.

TWO

Why You Need a Sales System

Stop and think about your last drive to the office, or to your local grocery store. Unless something unusual happened, you will likely struggle to remember the details.

There is a reason for that: because it will have been a journey you've taken dozens or hundreds of times before, your brain automates the task of getting you from one recognized location to another. You can travel many miles while your conscious mind is engaged in something completely different.

That's just one example, but it illustrates the power of systems and routines. The more we use them, the easier our lives become. We have a series of steps and know both the order in which they should be followed and the signs we should see along the way. That's true whether we are driving across coasts, painting houses, or writing books like this one. Each includes a list of activities that can be performed in a certain sequence. And they all get simpler with practice.

Selling to customers is no different. Just as you don't drive a different way to work each morning, neither should you approach your selling day as if you had never met with the buyer before. You should have a set of predictable steps to follow that will lead you from your first interaction to a finished order or account.

While the points I'm making here might seem fairly obvious, there are literally millions of sales-people out there who don't use established plans or programs. For them – and anyone who might be skeptical about the value of a structured selling approach – I want to provide some more concrete benefits to following a sales system. But first, there is a question I need to answer…

What Is a Sales System?

If you are new to sales, or haven't had much training in your profession, you might not be familiar with the idea of a sales system. So, what is it?

I once wondered the same thing. When I got my first job selling real estate, I just wanted to make some money. Back then the industry wasn't as sophisticated as it is now, and I certainly didn't have as much knowledge or experience as most of my colleagues did.

What I did have, though, was a ton of ambition and a desire to learn. So I set out to find ways to get more clients. What I learned through books and seminars is that most successful sales follow a predictable path. That's because the "buyer's journey" is based on simple psychology.

A sales system just helps you to plan, organize, and execute the right steps in the process. They'll normally include things like:

- Finding prospects in your target market
- Qualifying those prospects for their true buying potential
- Showing off your products and services so prospects understand their value
- Developing bids and presentations
- Negotiating with buyers and closing the sale

In that way, a sales system is really just a recipe

for various interactions that can be followed again and again.

These days there are dozens of well-known sales systems out there (including my *MODERN Sales System*, which I developed during my own career and have taught around the world). There are systems for phone selling, retail systems, and systems specific to individual industries or companies. Personally, I think a good sales system should work in almost *any* environment, but we'll get to that later.

With this short definition out of the way, let's move on to the reasons you need to be selling with an organized plan.

Using a System Makes You a Better Salesperson

I'll start with something that has become very clear to me, and to the companies that hire me to speak and train: when you follow a sales system, you become more effective at prospecting, qualifying, negotiating, and closing.

There are a lot of reasons for this, but the big one has to do with borrowed knowledge. Sales systems are developed by people like me who have decades of experience working with a variety of customers. We know what works because we have been in your shoes. When you stick to the blueprints we have provided, you aren't reinventing the wheel.

However, following a selling system would be valuable even if it was one you had developed yourself. That's because it forces you to be conscious about what you're doing and what you want to accomplish. It keeps you on track with your calls, emails, and meetings.

This is important for both new salespeople and experienced vets alike. Salespeople who are just getting started can avoid common mistakes and quickly integrate advanced tactics and ideas. Those who have been at it for a while can stop themselves from making common mistakes or getting complacent.

Years ago I was booked to speak at a conference full of people. The presenter before me was a professional athlete who had enjoyed a long and successful career. He talked about how when he was a child, scouts had noticed his size, talent, and quickness. However, even though he was already the biggest and fastest, his coaches drilled him endlessly on the skills and movements. They didn't want him to simply rely on his natural physical gifts because it would have put a lower ceiling on his potential.

Can you see the analogy to your sales career? You might have been born with good looks, charisma, and likability. But if you don't have basic selling skills (the kind you get from a sales system), your career is going to be driven by luck rather than effort. You won't have control of your own income or destiny.

I've met salespeople who were awkward. I've known others who had less than great educations or missing family connections. But they were able to make it because they had good plans and strategies to follow.

Sales Systems Stop You From Missing the Obvious

I take a lot of trips in my job, and my father was a pilot. As a result of either or both of these things, I have a small interest in aviation. One of the things I've learned in talking to professional pilots is that they rely on an almost endless number of checklists to guide them through any specific situation or scenario. From pre-flight checks to landing preparations, there are always steps to read out and follow.

Using checklists might seem unnecessary, especially in instances where the captain of an airliner might have tens of thousands of flight hours behind them. But really, that's the point. By looking at a written set of notes, they are forced to make sure they don't miss something so routine that they wouldn't otherwise think about it (like fueling up the plane, for example, or putting down the landing gear).

If that sounds absurd, consider that *those exact mistakes* have been made by flight crews in the past. That's what happens when people get tired or find themselves doing repetitive tasks. They switch off and miss details that turn out to be critical later.

You have surely noticed this in your own life. How often have you found yourself getting tired or distracted and then doing something silly? We've all had the experience of putting too much sugar into our coffee or missing an exit on the highway. We don't do these things because we are incompetent, but because it's easy for little day-to-day concerns to stop us from dialing in as carefully as we should to the task at hand.

It's one thing to waste a few minutes on the road or cut yourself shaving. It's another to blow a big sale or miss out on a chunk of money because you forgot to ask a question or go over an important benefit of your product or service. If you aren't following a sales system, that can happen without you even noticing.

Even the simplest sales usually involve a handful of steps or interactions that need to be followed. When you add in complex elements like proposals, contracts, or regulatory approvals, a sale can become complex very quickly. Start managing dozens of prospects or clients at once and it becomes almost certain that you'll miss something if you don't have the right guide in place.

Every time you forget to explain a selling point, leave out a term in your proposal, or forget to follow up with a customer the way you said you would, it does damage to your income and credibility. A good sales system stops you from making these kinds of little mistakes. It also frees you from using up your mental energy to worry about them so you can concentrate on the deal that's right in front of you.

A Sales System Keeps You in Sync With Your Customers

One sure sign of an underperforming salesperson is that they don't really listen to their prospects and customers – instead, they just think about what they are going to say next when the other person is speaking.

Naturally, active listening skills play a role in making you a stronger salesperson. However, I would argue that a good sales system can be a big help in this area, too.

When you don't go into a selling situation with a strategy, things can feel stressful. Mentally, you have to keep up with buyers while they are introducing twists and turns that weren't anticipated. You might find yourself scrambling to address objections about price, or have to explain features you haven't demonstrated yet.

These kinds of speed bumps can occur in the midst of any sale, of course, but they happen a lot less frequently when you're using a selling system. One reason has to do with the fact that you're following a structured plan that guides customers from one logical step to the next. You are taking control of the situation and giving them the right amount of information in just the right order. Because you aren't flying by the seat of your pants, the main points get covered and buyers are less likely to get confused or interrupt.

Another reason selling gets easier with a system has to do with fluency. Think back to your first days riding a bike or driving a car. In the beginning you had to think about each motion or movement. Over time, though, they became second nature and you could do either one while talking to a friend or singing along with the radio.

Selling is like that, too. When you're following a system, you know where you're going and what should happen at each stage in the game. You don't have to think ahead so intently, so you can listen carefully, take notes, and really focus on what customers are telling you. You aren't distracted and can devote all of your energy to finding the right product or service for the person sitting right in front of you.

People can tell when you're locked into their words and ideas. The more attention you pay, the more you learn about their wants and needs. Your listening builds trust and gives you the ammunition to go for the close later.

It's virtually impossible to be fully present and engaged when you're always worried about what you have to say to close a sale. But, when you're following a proven process, staying focused is the natural result of being relaxed and intentional.

Sales Systems Save Time and Increase Efficiency

Mediocre salespeople are happy just to close a deal. The best in the business do everything they can to get efficient because they know they only have a certain number of hours to sell each day and want to maximize their earnings.

It should be obvious that you're going to get more done if you are following a sales system than you would if you weren't. Having a process makes any task smoother and helps you to spot areas where effort is being wasted.

A salesperson who uses a plan will know, for example, that they need to learn all the relevant facts about a selling situation before moving into a presentation. So they'll collect information about other vendors, technical needs, budgetary concerns, delivery timeframes, and even decision-making authority before they bother to present a solution. Because of that, they won't have to go back later and find new answers that meet a faster timeframe, or give extra presentations because they didn't understand who had the authority to approve a purchase.

Those are little examples, but they creep up again and again throughout your week and over the course of your career. An organized salesperson might be able to get through a simple client meeting in 30 minutes with time to spare. One who doesn't know how to progress a sale from one stage to the next might flounder along for twice as long, wasting their own time and annoying the buyer along the way.

No matter what you do you'll never be able to invent more than 24 hours in a single day. By spending fewer of them on redundant tasks, and devoting the bulk of your schedule and energy to hot prospects rather than cold leads, you can go a long way toward joining the ranks of the top salespeople in your business or industry. Using a logical sales system allows you to get more from every hour.

You'll Earn More by Using a Sales System

The bottom line – and what a really good salesperson wants to know – is that the men and women who follow selling systems outearn the ones who don't. In fact, my experience tells me that the sales professionals who truly commit to a proven plan do much better than those who simply follow along because their employers make them.

It's not hard to understand why if you've paid attention in this chapter. A producer using a sales system is more informed and less prone to making mistakes. They don't overlook important steps or find themselves wasting time on trivial tasks. They pay close attention to their customers and enjoy more trust and credibility as a result.

Each of these benefits is enormous, but it's the way they work together that is truly amazing. If all of your efforts are focused and cohesive, there is a kind of synergy that kicks in. You stop being an average salesperson, bouncing from one task or potential contract to another, and start to realize compounding improvements over time. It gets easier to sell because you understand what it takes to move buyers through your sales pipeline and can handle the job more predictably.

Imagine what it would be like to know, more or less, that you could easily close the number of orders you need to achieve a bonus or win some sort of incentive. Think about what it would be like to never feel stress about what you'll need to tell a customer to win their account or secure an agreement. Best of all, envision yourself moving to close a sale without experiencing any anxiety over unknown objections.

If you're already using a proven sales system and working effectively, you don't have to imagine these things. If none of them seems realistic to you, then take that as a sign you need to start getting more organized with your sales efforts.

Although I feel like I've made a good case for the importance of a sales system, I think it's a good idea to look at the other side of the coin as well. In the next chapter we will briefly explore what you get when you *don't* have an organized process in place for generating sales.

THREE

What Happens When You Don't Have a
Sales System

What Happens When You Don't Have a Sales System

Sometimes the companies I train for will pair my presentations with fun outings and teambuilding activities. One client that stands out in my mind took his group of new sales hires to an escape room after a long day of learning.

I hadn't ever been to one of these establishments, but the concept is simple: teams are released into an environment with abstract clues that lead to a key or combination that sets them free. They have to escape before time runs out or a competing team makes it to their goal first.

What a great way to illustrate the power of

knowledge and planning. Imagine for a moment that I had my own escape room and could lock a salesperson into one of the chambers. On the other side of the wall I would have an identical room, but only one had a set of clear instructions. Which one would be likely to win? If I repeated the experiment dozens or hundreds of times, how divergent would the results become?

The producer who is using a system to turn opportunities into commission checks will come out ahead of their peers and competitors who aren't following a plan every time. There might be instances where luck and circumstances make a sales system unnecessary, but even in those situations it isn't going to hurt – you'll just get to your goal faster.

Because understanding this point is so crucial to your development as a salesperson, I want to be sure it comes through as clearly as possible. So in this brief chapter I'm going to explore some of the outcomes that are inevitable when you don't have a sales system in place…

Without a Sales System You Make Predictable Mistakes

I have trained and presented at hundreds of companies around the world, and have met thousands upon thousands of salespeople in the process. As I've heard their stories, worked with them in the field and given them advice, I've noticed there are certain errors that pop up again and again. I'm not referring to "bad luck" circumstances that seem to come out of nowhere, but the entirely avoidable blunders we all commit before we know better.

It's a fact of life that many of our most crucial lessons seem obvious in hindsight. Until they are pointed out, however, it's difficult to identify them, much less correct our own behavior.

Builders follow blueprints because they lead to predictable results and eliminate costly or dangerous mistakes. The same thing happens with selling. In the first chapter I pointed out that a good sales system will have been developed by a veteran in the field and then tested and refined over the years. It will be proven in all the ways that matter. If you want to avoid common errors that can cost you a ton of money, then use a solid strategy as the foundation of your career and philosophy.

When You Don't Have a Sales Strategy You Spend Time Chasing the Wrong Prospects

I'm going to dig into the aspects of a good sales system in the next chapter, but one thing all of the strongest ones have in common is a focus on separating good sales opportunities from others that only look good. In other words, to identify the accounts you have a good chance of winning.

This is a crucial step in the selling process because it stops you from devoting time and resources on a lost cause. We all know what it's like to get your hopes (and hours) invested in a deal that never comes to fruition. It's incredibly frustrating. Imagine what it would be like to not only get that time back, but to have spent it working with buyers who are moving toward a close rather than wasting your time.

When you lose entire days and weeks writing proposals, making follow-up calls, and otherwise chasing down prospects who don't have a real intention of buying from you, then you're hurt twice. The first pinch is felt when you don't turn that effort into a commission check. The second comes when you realize you could have identified a better opportunity and closed it.

You can't get wasted time back, and a habit of spending too much of it on non-viable leads can be a career killer. That's a risk you run when you aren't following a sales system.

Making Sales Takes More Time

There are a lot of things you can get done without the proper instructions. For example, you could use the right tools and ingredients to bake a cake, change a tire, or build a birdhouse. But that doesn't mean the job will be easy or that you'll feel good about the results.

That analogy sums up the way I feel when I see a salesperson struggling their way through a client meeting or demonstration without the right skills or process. They'll occasionally close some business, but it isn't going to be fun. Moreover, there is a chance the customer won't get what they wanted or needed, which could lead to dissatisfaction, more customer service time, or reduced selling and referral opportunities in the future.

When I'm teaching my *MODERN Sales System*, I like to remind attendees that every sale has a beginning, middle, and an end. There's no way around that. You have to find prospects, find out about their needs, present a solution, and then close the sale. That can take seconds or years, but each phase is going to happen.

When you have to stop yourself, repeat portions of your presentation, or address questions that should have been addressed earlier, you are being wasteful. You're giving away your time, exhausting your customers, and taking away minutes you could be using to close another deal. Without a sales system, you'll run into these issues again and again.

Making a sale is about helping your customer and getting a result. However, building a strong sales career is all about being focused and efficient. That's simply not possible if you are devoting too much time to every possibility or interaction.

Your Closing Ratios Decline When You Don't Use a Sales System

In the last chapter I explained how using a sales system lets you devote all of your focus and energy into a customer who needs your help. When that happens, they respond in kind, giving you more information and becoming more willing to listen to the products and services you offer them.

It's only natural that the opposite happens when you aren't as organized as you could be. You end up concentrating on your sales pitch or some point you wanted to make rather than the background information a buyer is giving you. Consciously or subconsciously, they'll recognize that you aren't paying as much attention to them and feel hesitant about working with you. They will wonder whether you actually understand what they are looking for, or are simply presenting ideas to boost your income.

That would be bad enough, but there is also a carryover effect. Consider this: when you have good rapport with the customer, and there is lots of give and take, your confidence is sky high. You are following a system that leads you predictably toward a higher income and feel good about what you're doing.

Now think about the way selling feels when your confidence is low. It's like trying to hike through wet concrete. With each missed opportunity or declined proposal, you deflate a little more. The cycle begins to feed itself and your prospects for winning new business start to circle the drain.

In other words, using a sales system to follow a process and listen to your customers nets you more accounts from the opportunities you generate. Taking a disorganized approach to selling prevents you from closing as many deals as you can.

Without a sales system you waste time on poor prospects, which means you generate fewer opportunities because you aren't organized. At the same time, you also close a lower percentage of the leads you *do* identify. That double penalty can be a weight that drags your paycheck down for years or even decades.

Without a Strategy You Lose Sales and Don't Know Why

Although I tend to focus on the fact that a sales system keeps you doing the right things and moves your prospects through a predictable sales pipeline, a side effect is that you get better information at every stage. You understand more of what you hear and see, and can tell when things are getting away from you.

I always know when a sales professional has been using a proven plan because they know exactly what is and isn't working for a given client and interaction. Because they do such a good job of prospecting, qualifying, presenting, and closing in a consistent way, they can pinpoint precisely the moment when a sale has been lost. They know that a customer doesn't have the money or buying authority needed to complete a contract. Or they can tell when the solution they have presented doesn't meet the needs of the situation.

This is valuable insight for couple of reasons. First, it stops them from wasting time on poor prospects (as I've already described). Even more importantly, it gives them the information needed to improve their approach in the future. For example, they can prospect differently, tweak their demonstrations, or use new negotiating strategies.

Contrast that with the way most mediocre salespeople talk. When the deal doesn't close they'll often admit they have no idea why. They'll chalk it up to bad luck even though there isn't usually any such thing in the world of commission selling. What they think of as an uncontrollable event actually came down to a problem that should have been anticipated or a question that was unasked.

We all lose sales sometimes. However, it's much better to learn from our missteps and mistakes than it is to repeat them – painfully and expensively – again and again.

You Can't Join the Best Without Adopting Their Habits

As I've pointed out, decades of work in this business have taught me that salespeople who use systems make more money. It shouldn't be a huge shock, then, that salespeople who don't follow a plan tend to make less. That's just the way math works.

When you're relying on luck to produce new accounts, or going into every situation "winging it," you are still likely to get some things to go your way. You'll wander into some situations where a client is ready to buy, or where your product or service is such a good fit that the sale is never really in doubt.

However, that's going to happen less often than it would if you are more prepared, and you're going to find fewer prospects, referrals, and repeat customers than you would if you were following a proven sales system. Extend those results out for a while and you'll understand why you might have the occasional big year or quarter, but you're never going to be a top performer.

In one business after another, I've seen that the award-winners bringing home the biggest checks are not only working with prospects in an organized way, but are continually refining their approaches to get the most from the sales system they employ. If you want to join their ranks, why wouldn't you make the effort to do the things they do and follow the same approach?

Hopefully, these two short chapters have convinced you that there isn't any good reason to avoid using a sales system if you want to do more than get by in your career. That brings up the obvious question: which sales system should you follow?

That's a topic I'll explore in the next chapter…

FOUR

How to Choose the Right Sales System

If I haven't yet convinced you of the need to choose a sales system to help you find more customers and close more accounts, then you can stop reading now. You aren't interested enough in making money to benefit from good advice.

On the other hand, if you've decided you would like to organize your selling efforts – not to mention earn awards and increase your income – then the next step is choosing the sales system that's right for you.

As important as this decision is, I'm not going to spend a huge amount of time on this topic. There are a couple of reasons I don't want to go overboard in discussing your choice of a sales system.

The first is philosophical. As the creator of *The*

MODERN Sales System, I'm obviously a little bit biased. I spent many years trying, learning, and even teaching other sales systems before developing something new that I felt shared the best traits of the others with a unique twist. I won't pretend I want you to try another one when I think mine is superior.

There is also a practical reason for me not to dwell on this topic. Many of the salespeople reading this book will not have had the option of selecting their own sales system. A manager will have given them a blueprint to follow, and usually one that is being used throughout an entire organization.

If you've been assigned *The MODERN Sales System* to learn, then you're in luck because you've got a tool that can help you grow your income exponentially. If your sales manager has given you another similar program to follow, I won't hold it against you and you'll probably be just fine. In either case you can either browse my thoughts in this chapter or move on to the next section.

However, if you're still in the process of finding the best sales system to meet your needs, then let's look at some criteria that should matter.

The Best Sales Systems Are Easy to Learn and Use

When you're talking about core concepts, selling isn't complicated. You have to reach out to prospects, find out if they are a good fit for what you sell, and then present your solutions. When you do this well, it will work more often than not.

Despite that reality, there are some incredibly complicated selling systems out there. I have personally seen a few that have more than twenty steps. These kinds of schemes might work well on paper, but they fall apart in the real world. That's because customer interactions are fluid, and can move quickly. Sometimes you think you're ready for one phase of a sale only to find out you have to retreat. Or you come across a buyer who is in a hurry and spends much less time than expected on an activity that normally takes longer.

My own sales system has six simple steps. That makes it easy to learn and practical to use. I'm very skeptical of plans and formulas that go very far beyond that. What are their creators adding in to make the selling process so much longer and more complex? And what are the odds that salespeople are actually using those extra steps effectively rather than talking themselves (and their customers) out of finished deals?

A good sales system is like a diet or a time-management strategy. If you can't sum it up in a few quick sentences, then you are probably over-complicating things and hurting your effectiveness in the process.

A Good Sales System Should Be Versatile

As I mentioned earlier, some sales systems are designed for specific environments (like retail, auto sales, etc). I can understand the desire to work with a set of tools and terminologies that are industry-specific, but I don't think it's wise to follow a plan that isn't versatile.

Hyper-specific sales systems are usually predicated on unique circumstances. That makes them useful in one context, but hard to follow when conditions change. For example, I once had someone tell me about a set of steps their car dealers were supposed to follow to deal with customers who were coming on the lot. One of the steps involved asking a long series of questions to help the buyer zero in on a specific make, model, and color that was already on the lot. That information would then be used later in the process to set up a close.

It was a bit manipulative, but it could work in some instances. However, when internet shopping became a trend and customers started showing up already knowing exactly what they wanted to drive off the lot, it fell to pieces. It wasn't flexible enough to withstand the shift in the buying process.

A stronger sales system wouldn't be so dependent on one single activity. A versatile strategy is one that is built on principles rather than gimmicks. It's the difference between knowing all the streets in a town and having a set of directions scribbled on a napkin. When you have a system that teaches you how to sell, you aren't reliant on the little details. When you don't, you have to hope everything goes your way.

You Should Be Able to Use Your Sales System With a CRM

As I have noted in virtually all my books and most of the seminars I have ever delivered, good note-taking and record-keeping is vital to your sales career. If you aren't organized, you can't keep information straight, and sales opportunities will fall through the cracks.

For that reason, I'm a big believer in using your sales system and CRM software closely together. The sales system keeps you moving in the right direction while the CRM keeps you from missing chances to make contact or close a new account.

Ideally, you would choose your sales system first

and CRM second. What matters most, however, is that the two work well together. This shouldn't be an issue unless (as I discussed above) your sales plan is overly complicated or inflexible. When that's the case it might be difficult or impossible to find tools that allow you to track the kind of minutia the system calls for.

You can have a selling system without a CRM in place, but I don't recommend you use either without the other. Knowing that, you should ensure they can be coordinated in a way that makes you as efficient as possible.

The Three Costs of a Sales System

Learning a sales system usually entails some sort of expense, which can be very small or very significant. One thing you have to keep in mind is that the costs can add up quickly once you start looking beyond the obvious numbers.

Whether you are choosing a sales system for yourself or for an entire department, you might want to invest in books, seminars, or intensive training to pick up the fundamentals and see them applied in realistic situations. That price tag has to be considered, but it's usually a relatively minor consideration.

Moving beyond the obvious you'll want to think

about the expenses associated with continual training or advanced modules. Some companies will offer you a very reasonable rate on an initial program, but charge you a huge fee to learn additional techniques (including some to help you plug the holes in their sales system). Depending on the costs and the number of people or lessons that have to be included, this could make the project more expensive than you initially realized.

By far, though, the biggest cost associated with implementing a sales system has to do with the time and effort it takes to learn. A simple sales plan that is rooted in common-sense activities can be mastered within weeks. That means you (or your team) can be up and running very quickly. You'll start to reap the benefits and see a positive ROI.

Conversely, if a sales system is overly complicated it might be difficult for a salesperson or department to catch on. Then, it isn't just that business takes longer to pick up, but that leads and opportunities can be bungled in the meantime. In that situation, quotas might be missed and the long-term health of the business could suffer.

The true cost of a sales system can be higher than anticipated if you aren't careful. Make sure you know what you're paying for and committing to before you make a final decision.

Your Sales System Needs to Generate Results

The bottom line on a sales system is that it has to make you better at your job. If it doesn't, then why bother learning it at all?

If you're in a position where you can choose your own sales system, or recommend one to your team, then I would encourage you to check out a few different choices. Judge them on the criteria I've laid out in this short chapter, but also speak with a few accomplished sales professionals you trust to get their opinion. They should be able to tell you whether they've known someone who has followed it and what their results were like.

You can also talk with someone who teaches the system you want to learn and check out supporting materials online or in books. A good sales system won't have been invented out of nothing; the creator will have a long track record of work behind them and a rationale for the way they've put together the various steps that are supposed to lead you toward more clients and bigger commission checks.

Never forget that selling is a results business.

What's flashy or fun isn't always the most effective, and what works in the real world doesn't always carry a high price or require a great deal of hype to sell. Make a decision that's based on common sense and future earnings. If you aren't sure, shop around until you find a sales system that seems right (or if you want the best, just buy one of my books and start using it).

A Word to Executives and Sales Managers

I've had a bit of fun in this chapter around my obvious preference for my own sales system. However, I don't want to wrap the section up without reminding you that choosing a program for your company or department to follow is a very big decision. Your future paychecks and career prospects are riding on it, and so are those of your employees.

It's an unfortunate fact that some of the men and women working in the sales training industry are better at pitching themselves than they ever were at finding customers in their former careers. As a consequence, the sales systems they develop and name after themselves aren't as well thought out or tested as they could be.

As sales professionals, we can ironically be more

vulnerable to a smooth pitch or slick presentation. We can occasionally make the mistake of buying sports cars when regular trucks and station wagons can do the trick with lower costs and less maintenance.

The point I'm trying to make here is that you should choose a sales system that's easy to learn, follow, and master. It should perform in a variety of situations, help to generate real-world accounts, and help your team to sell in a focused and ethical way. You owe it to yourself and your producers to not settle for anything less than that.

FIVE

Learning Your Sales System

It would be nice if simply selecting the right sales system would be enough to instantly boost your income. However, if you really want to sell more, you're going to have to make it a part of your day-to-day working routine. That means you have to not just learn it, but integrate it into all of your activities.

This can be a little bit harder than it sounds, particularly if you have established or ingrained habits. In most areas of selling it's the experienced veterans who have a big advantage. When it comes to learning and implementing a new sales system, though, things are easiest for new recruits. That's because they don't have to stop doing what they were before.

For example, when I'm teaching *The MODERN Sales System*, one of my biggest challenges is getting reps to take their time and move through the steps properly. So many of them want to rush ahead to the close. However, the process I have laid out for them is structured as it is for specific reasons.

For instance, if you don't qualify a customer and figure out what they need from you (the "measure" and "organize" steps), you're always going to get resistance when trying to win new business. It's easier for someone who hasn't made many sales to see the common sense in that notion. But, for a sales professional who has already been making a living in their job for a while, it can be a tough transition... even if they want to be earning more than they currently are.

The point I'm trying to make here is that an open mind and a little bit of patience are your best tools when trying to master a new sales system. You might not get things perfectly right in the first couple of weeks, and you may have to rethink some old patterns. However, if you're willing to stick with it you can accomplish all the amazing things I've already brought up.

With that in mind, let's look at what you can do to master your chosen sales system faster.

Know the Steps and Speak the Language

Given the benefits that come with mastering a selling system, it only makes sense to learn the one you choose inside and out. Don't just read through the steps once or twice and assume it's going to help you to get results – commit them to memory so deeply that you could recite them on cue without hesitation if you had to.

Obviously, no one other than your sales manager is going to ask you to list off the steps of your sales system randomly. But, by preparing yourself in this way, you can make sure you have the tools you need to work through real customer interactions.

There's a difference between knowing *about* your sales system and actually *knowing it* inside and out. When you have made the effort to truly learn it, you don't just have the steps down, but also get the reasoning for each one and the overall order. You become confident with the plan and know that it's a part of your routine and mindset.

One way to foster this kind of familiarity is to "speak the language" of your sales system. When talking about opportunities with your colleagues, use the language of the plan. That will help to cut down on confusion when collaborating with others and seeking their advice. It will also reinforce what you have learned again and again.

Give Yourself Visual Reminders

Whether you've been using a sales system for a few hours or a few decades, you can always benefit from having it at the front of your mind. One way to accomplish that is to leave yourself visual reminders of the steps and key concepts in your field of vision.

For instance, I often visit client offices where students of mine have placed MODERN posters in their meeting rooms. Others keep small postcard-sized learning aids at their desks. These aren't meant to teach them my sales system, but to remind them that they should always be striving to work the steps thoroughly.

You could even use this concept to prepare yourself for client meetings and presentations. If you haven't been using a sales system for long, bring a few notes on a sheet of paper, or set a notification for your phone. These are little things, but they can help you to stay on track when you're feeling rushed or pressured.

Earlier I described a sales system as being similar to a recipe. Whether you cook frequently or not, you have probably had the experience of making dinner for a date or for some family members. If you wanted to impress them, you probably took a few moments to read through the directions and prepare your ingredients before getting started. Why would you do anything less when preparing to work with a live customer who could help you make more money?

Use Training as a Reinforcing Tool

When you were in school, your teacher didn't show you how to add, subtract, and multiply numbers once and then move on. Instead, she took weeks and weeks teaching you these skills so they would stay with you for a lifetime. She knew that you had to be taught the same concepts more than once if they were going to sink in.

As adults, we have the freedom to choose whether to keep learning or not. That means most of us don't spend our evenings and weekends practicing equations anymore, but it also means we are free to neglect our own development and income if we aren't careful.

I've had clients hire me to train *The MODERN Sales System* numerous different times for the same groups. That isn't because their teams aren't smart or haven't mastered the basics. Instead, it's because they know there is big power in repetition and reinforcement. It sometimes helps to be reminded of what we're doing, and why, even if we already grasp the basics.

After many of the sessions, students have approached me to say they are thankful they've gotten the chance to learn my sales system all over again. Most say they get something new out of it a second or third time. Even though the core principles never change, their understanding of the underlying tools and steps does. They are happy to keep giving me their time and attention because they know they'll make more money after I leave.

Whatever sales system you are using, don't let training be a one-and-done event. Check out seminars, webinars, books, and other resources to improve your knowledge and make it easier to put those ideas to work. You'll get a great deal from simply figuring out the steps of a plan, but real and lasting improvement comes with a commitment that goes on for longer.

Use Your Sales System to Diagnose New Accounts and Missed Chances

One of the best and most overlooked ways to master a sales system is by applying it retroactively to selling situations. In other words, go back *after* a customer has said "yes" or "no" and move through the steps to figure out why.

In some cases, you might stumble upon truths that weren't obvious when you were in the midst of the sale. For instance, it's very common to discover that you may have rushed through a phase in the process or failed to ask an important qualifying question. Maybe you'll see that a tough negotiation was set up by a demonstration that didn't hit the right points, or that you have to be prospecting for different accounts if you want to get higher margins.

Thinking through these kinds of "after action reports" can be beneficial in a number of ways. For one thing, they help you to understand where your wins are coming from, as well as your own strengths and weaknesses as a producer. And, they can help you make smarter decisions in the future so you become more efficient.

In a more immediate sense, though, this activity integrates the language of your sales system into your daily thought. It ensures you not only under-stand the big ideas, but can apply them in real-life situations where a customer is in front of you. It can even give you clues about the advantages and disadvantages of a sales system you are using, and how you can bring it together with your style, the products and services you sell, and the situations you face.

You don't have to obsess over every new account or missed opportunity, but you should regularly review your progress – either alone or with a sales manager. That way, you'll always be getting stronger while at the same time figuring out which parts of your sales system you are proficient with and which steps need a bit of further review or training.

Practice and Role Play in the Office

One of the great things about having an entire sales department learn a new system is that the reps can practice using terminology and techniques on each other in a low-stress environment. That makes for increased cooperation and better learning retention because everyone is actually using the plan rather than simply seeing it in a book or a slide.

I would encourage you to work these kinds of drills and practice activities as often as you can. Set aside half an hour in the afternoon to go over some points with a colleague. Introduce different scenarios and sales meetings. Try phrasing questions and ideas that are part of your selling system in different ways with a friend or mentor after you've met with a client.

Naturally, each of these gives you a way to smooth out your delivery and make the sales system your own. However, they also give you the opportunity to think critically about what you're doing and explain your insights to other people. As a longtime author, coach, and presenter I can tell you there is truth to the idea that you don't truly understand the subject until you have to teach it to someone else. Doing so fires up a different part of your mind and makes the information you have retained more useful.

I also want to point out that there is a practical aspect to this advice. As beneficial as it is to have a sales system to work with, you don't necessarily want to be learning the basics while you are presenting to clients and have your earnings on the line. In other words, it's best to make your mistakes in a situation where you can try again and again with a colleague rather than blowing a sale and missing out on a commission you could have earned.

Of course, that notion will only take you so far. If you really want to learn, master, and profit from your sales system, you are going to need to use it in real selling situations as often as possible.

Practice Makes Perfect

No matter how much you learn, how many seminars you attend, and what kind of visual aids you put around your office, there isn't any way to get good with a sales system that doesn't involve meeting live prospects. You just have to go through dozens and dozens of calls or meetings until you feel absolutely comfortable that you not only understand the steps but can apply them in a way that comes to you naturally.

The bad news about this is that you may not feel comfortable selling in a different way when you're first getting started. I've had numerous professionals tell me they felt like MODERN was slowing them down in the beginning, or that they felt a little awkward following a blueprint rather than simply listening to their instincts or sticking with old habits. In other words, there is likely to be a learning curve.

The good news, though, is that these feelings tend to pass pretty quickly. Once you get fluent with your selling system, you can move quite naturally and effortlessly from one step or phase of a sale to another. If anything, following a plan can actually make you feel freer. That's because you'll know what you need to do to get your customer to agree, and don't have to worry you'll miss something important. You can focus on them, gather information, provide benefits, and know where it's all going without being overwhelmed.

Once you've chosen a sales system, you have to decide you're going to master it. Then, you have to put in the hours of work to learn the steps (and the transitions between them) so thoroughly that they feel as if you had invented them yourself.

Practice makes perfect. When you put in the work needed, you move beyond the point of "using" a sales system and into the realm of mastery. That's when the magic starts to happen.

SIX

Sales System Mastery

In this short book I've walked you through a number of steps you have to follow to understand the value of a selling system, choose one that will work for you, and then put it to good use. If you can take that advice to heart, you'll end up at a stage I call *sales system mastery*.

This is a level I reached in my own selling career decades ago, and I've had the honor of guiding thousands of others to the same place. It's not a formal designation, of course. You won't receive a certificate in the mail. Nonetheless, you'll know you've achieved it when a couple of important things happen: *you start to feel more confident in your ability to sell and see your income increase dramatically.*

I would argue those are some of the best rewards you can get for anything.

What makes sales system mastery so valuable is that it feels unconscious. Even though you may have started out trying to memorize a few steps or understand why you have to take time that feels unnecessary when you're trying to make sales, all of your work and dedication begin to pay off very quickly.

At this stage you start to become a supercharged salesperson. You can find more qualified prospects than you ever have before. When delivering a presentation, you can immediately notice whether customers are engaged with you or not. It feels as if negotiating and closing new sales is simpler than ever, and referrals are coming your way left and right.

These are all wonderful benefits, but you don't get them for free. Instead, they show up when you have followed a predictable plan that leads you in the right direction.

To put things another way, this short book is a kind of sales system itself. Let's take a moment to review the steps I've given you to follow:

- Understand that selling systems help you

organize your activities and be both
more efficient and effective.

- Know that when you aren't using a sales
  system you run the risk of wasting time
  and money you don't have to lose.
- Choose a sales system that fits your
  business and personality while allowing
  you the chance to make record-breaking
  commissions.
- Learn and practice your sales system
  until it becomes a part of you, and then
  keep refining your approach so it
  becomes an unconscious skill.

If you can follow those guidelines, you have what it takes to learn and master a sales system that will help you to double, triple, or even quadruple the amount of money you're making now. And, if you're going to do the hard work of contacting clients and convincing them to buy from you, why wouldn't you want to do it in the easiest and highest-paying way possible?

Although I love my sales system and am proud of it, I put this short book together because I want every sales professional to be following some sort of proven blueprint for success and improvement. I don't want to see anyone make the all too common mistakes so many people do when trying to win new accounts.

Sales system mastery is about taking control of your paycheck and career. It's using the resources that are available to ensure no one else has an advantage over you when trying to win the business you need.

I am a big believer in sales systems and by this point I hope you are, too. Find the one that can help you take your career to the next level and then make the most of it. Once you do, you won't be able to stop telling other people about the power of sales system mastery!

SEVEN

Free Gift: The MODERN Sales System Preview

Thank you investing your valuable time in my book. I hope you found the advice I have on sales systems to be valuable, and that you'll use what you've learned to either find a sales system that works for you or get more from the one you already have.

In finishing up the first draft of this short title, I found myself with a dilemma. When I showed the writing to a handful of clients and colleagues, their feedback was unanimous: I needed to include some information about *The MODERN Sales System* for readers to follow.

"Carl, you already told them why a sales system is so important and how to use one," they told me. "Why wouldn't you introduce your own?"

The best answer, I suppose, was that I didn't

want to blatantly promote my own selling system in a short guide that's focused on the value of using *any* of them (I already have another book devoted exclusively to MODERN). And yet, I do think there is some value in describing my approach here. Not only is my plan good for a variety of industries and selling situations, but it might be helpful for those who don't already have a sales system to use and want to see an example of what a working plan looks like.

In the end, I decided there isn't any reason not to give you a free look at the tool that has helped me – not to mention hundreds of my clients – earn millions of dollars in sales commissions. And, I reminded myself that it's my book and I can promote something I believe in if I want to.

So, feel free to read on or skip over this no-cost guide to my blueprint for growing your business and income. Either way, as a big "thank you" for sharing your time with me, I want to present an overview of *The MODERN Sales System…*

An Overview of *The MODERN Sales System*

The MODERN Sales System is designed to guide you from your first contact with a new potential customer or client through a successful close. It consists of six easy-to-remember steps, as denoted by each letter of the word:

M – Measure the Selling Situation

O – Organize Your Client's Needs

D – Demonstrate Your Solutions

E – Engage the Mind and Senses

R – Review the Selling Situation

N – Negotiate and Close the Sale

While there are six steps to the system, they really come in three pairs. In early versions of my books, I liked to express them as MO-DE-RN. I've decided to leave the extra divisions in newer copies in order to make it easier on the eyes, but each of the six steps has a natural partner.

Let me explain. In the first part of the sale, you'll **Measure** and **Organize**. Or more plainly, you'll get to know your customer, let them get to know you, and find out about their needs. You find a prospect and ask targeted questions until you feel sure you understand what they need, why they are buying, and who has the power to make a decision.

From there, you **Demonstrate** and **Engage**, showing customers solutions to the problems you learned about in the first two steps. During this stage of the sale you show off a solution, high-lighting the benefits of your product or service that are most relevant to the challenges your customer has in front of them. And, you give them the chance to take emotional ownership of what you have to sell so they almost can't wait to buy it.

And finally, you **Review** and **Negotiate** to complete the sale. Although salespeople tend to worry and overthink the end of the selling process, in my system it happens quite naturally. Because you have done a little extra work earlier in the sale, things go more smoothly when it's time to reach an agreement. That means faster closing, less fighting, and better margins.

Naturally, I explain each of these selling phases in much greater depth in my book and seminars, but remember that the six steps of MODERN are really just three parts of a sale – the beginning, the middle, and the end.

The Two Rules for Using My Sales System

Because my sales system is built on the idea of simplicity, and because I never liked being bossed around myself, there are only two rules you have to follow to make MODERN work for you. However, both of them are incredibly important to its effectiveness. If you break one, you aren't going to hurt my feelings, but you probably are going to hurt your commission check.

The first rule is to try not to skip steps. Each of the six segments, as laid out in the MODERN acronym, represent phases of your interaction with the customer. Ignoring any of them will disrupt your path to the sale. As you get familiar with the system itself, you'll be able to see how one flows into another naturally. But for now, it's enough to say that you can't jump from the first step to the last any more than you would put frosting on a cake before you've baked it.

The second rule builds upon the first: if you can't move forward, move backward. That is, if you get resistance from your customer while trying to move them through the sales process, it's an indication you haven't performed one of the preceding steps thoroughly enough.

For instance, if you're trying to show a product in the Demonstrate step and the client isn't interested, then you probably haven't qualified their needs well enough in the Organize step. Or, if they're giving you a hard time in the Negotiate phase, then you might not have built up enough value in the Demonstrate and Engage steps.

I give a lot more context for these rules in my

book, but for this short overview just bear in mind that you can't skip steps, and that if you can't go forward you go back.

As with any good set of rules, however, these two come with an exception. If, at any point, the client says to you "I'd like to buy," without beating you up over price, then throw these steps out of the window and write up the order. If someone tries to buy from you and you refer them to your six-step selling process, you aren't just abusing my training, you're in the wrong job.

Why MODERN Works

I have been teaching my approach to selling for two decades, and it has been used successfully by thousands of salespeople around the world. Why has *The MODERN Sales System* been so effective for so many people? I think there are three important reasons.

First, it's very simple. As I mentioned before, many systems have a lot of complicated steps. Mine recognizes that nearly every successful sale is the result of a predictable process with a beginning, middle, and end. By simply following the six steps as they're outlined, almost any producer can find themselves selling more than they ever have before.

Second, *The MODERN Sales System* is organic.

By "organic," I don't mean that it's free of pesticides, (although it is), but rather that it is the product of years of testing and experience. Unlike many other systems, which have been devised in classrooms and trainers' minds, MODERN has been proven again and again by real salespeople in dozens of industries, all over the world. So what you find isn't a theory of how customers might buy from you, it's a blueprint for what works.

And finally, *The MODERN Sales System* focuses on the buyer, not the salesperson. It recognizes that selling is something that we do *with* the customer, not *to* the customer. This isn't just to make us feel good, although you will feel better about your work if you're doing the right thing. It turns out that we can sell more, and make a lot more money, by keeping our attention where it belongs – on the needs and wants of those who buy from us. By doing our best to help them, we help ourselves. My good friend Bill Brooks once observed that "successful people have a level and depth of wisdom about their area of endeavor that no one else has."

The MODERN Sales System is aimed at helping you to understand the sales process, and to make you a wiser and more successful producer along the way. How well will it work for you? That's largely up to you, but I'll leave you with a quote from one of my best clients. He's a top producer in his industry, earning well over half a million dollars each year. One afternoon, he sent me a simple, one-line note that was probably the best compliment I could have ever hoped for. It said, "Carl, please don't teach your MODERN Sales System to my competitors."

Want to Know More About *The MODERN Sales System*?

If you're looking for a pathway to more sales, higher margins, and less stress I invite you to check out my book, available in paperback, hardcover, and electronic versions on Amazon.com:

My Book

Additionally, information on my seminars and training programs can be found at **Carl-Henry.com**.

Good luck in your selling career!

About the Author

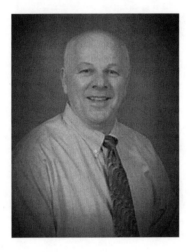

Carl Henry has been training and coaching sales professionals for 20+ years. He is the author of more than one dozen books, and has spoken for hundreds on companies on six different continents.

You can learn more about Carl and his work at www.carlhenry.com.

More Books by Carl Henry

More Books by Carl Henry

The MODERN Sales System
   15 Hot Tips to Supercharge Your Sales Career
   The PEOPLE Approach to Customer Service
   Hiring Top Talent for Sales
   Trade Show Selling
   The 5 POWER Presentation Steps
   52 Things Every Sales Manager Should Know
   High Energy Sales Thoughts
   Sell Something Everyday
   Overcoming Sales Objections
   Recharge Your Sales Career
   21 Career Transformation Tips

Made in the USA
Columbia, SC
24 June 2023

18780333R10039